REMEMBERING SEVEN PROPHETS

Ezra Taft Benson

REMEMBERING SEVEN PROPHETS

Ezra Taft Benson

MEMORIES OF FRANCIS M. GIBBONS
AS TOLD TO DANIEL BAY GIBBONS

Sixteen Stones Press
HOLLADAY, UTAH

Copyright © 2015 by Daniel Bay Gibbons

All rights reserved. No part of this publication may be reproduced, distributed or transmitted in any form or by any means, including photocopying, recording, or other electronic or mechanical methods, without the prior written permission of the publisher, except in the case of brief quotations embodied in critical reviews and certain other noncommercial uses permitted by copyright law.
Book layout, typography, and cover design ©2015 by Julie G. Gibbons. Photo credits: all cover photographs from the private collection of Francis M. Gibbons, used by permission. Sixteen Stones Press logo design by Marina Telezar.

Sixteen Stones Press
Publisher website: www.sixteenstonespress.com

Ezra Taft Benson
(Remembering Seven Prophets, Book 4)
by Daniel Bay Gibbons

Paperback ISBN 978-1-942640-10-3
eBook ISBN 978-0-9906387-4-2

TABLE OF CONTENTS

Remembering Seven Prophets 1

Chronology of the Life of President Ezra Taft Benson 5

"A portrait of President Benson" 11

"His birth was considered a great miracle" 15

"Two Prophets walked out of the same farmland" 17

"He became a man at age twelve" 19

"Bunkmates on either side of him died" 21

"A beautiful girl drove by in a sports car" 24

"Our Benson" 26

"The young couple decided against marrying" 29

"A striking contrast" 30

"An exemplary Latter-day Saint family" 32

"The Scoutmaster shaved his head" 33

"The cabin itself was a sacred place" 35

"Cities leveled by intense bombing" 37

"If the invitation comes in the proper spirit, you ought to accept" 39

"A modern-day Joseph in Pharaoh's Kingdom" 40

"To open doors for the Church" 42

"He cultivated a sense of family" 46

"He learned to think on his feet" 47

"He occasionally told a good story" 48

"We'll see if your spiritual antenna is up" 50

"Cooperation between two future Church Presidents" 54

"The prophetic mantle" 57

"No empty chairs" 58

"What's best for the Kingdom?" 61

"I look upon you as a true friend" 62

"Poise and self-control" 63

"No weapon that is formed against thee shall prosper" 64

About the Author 65

Index 66

REMEMBERING SEVEN PROPHETS

This collection of reminiscences about the life of President Ezra Taft Benson, the thirteenth President of The Church of Jesus Christ of Latter-day Saints, is part of a larger work entitled *Remembering Seven Prophets*. This work is the fruit of more than eighty hours of interviews I conducted with my father, Francis M. Gibbons, between the years 2001 to 2011, and then another dozen hours of interviews conducted between July and December of 2014 following my return from presiding over the Russia Novosibirsk Mission of the Church.

"A Plutarch to the Presidents of the Church"

Now in his ninety-fourth year, Francis M. Gibbons is perhaps the greatest student on the lives of the Presidents of the Church in this dispensation. He has two unique qualifications to speak and write about the Prophets.

First, over the past forty-five years, my father has become "a Plutarch to the Presidents of the Church." This unusual phrase has reference to Plutarch, the ancient Greek writer, who became the most famous biographer in history, the "Father of Biography." Many years ago my father shared with my mother his special aspiration to become "a Plutarch to the Presidents of the Church, and through their lives to write the history of the Church." If any man or woman deserves the title "Plutarch to the Presidents of the Church," it is my father, Francis M. Gibbons. Over the past four decades he has become, by far, the most prolific writer of biographies of the Presidents of the Church, writing a full-length biography of every Prophet from Joseph Smith to Gordon B. Hinckley. Dad's biographies of the Prophets have been very popular, selling many hundreds of thousands of copies. Thirteen of his presidential biographies have been included in Brigham Young University's list of "Sixty Significant Mormon Biographies." He has truly become "a Plutarch to the Presidents of the Church."

"A Scribe to the Prophets"

Second, my father has been a personal witness and observer of the character of the last seven Presidents of the Church:

Presidents Joseph Fielding Smith, Harold B. Lee, Spencer W. Kimball, Ezra Taft Benson, Howard W. Hunter, Gordon B. Hinckley, and Thomas S. Monson. He knew these men personally. He worked with them. While serving from 1970 to 1986 as the secretary to the First Presidency and later as a member of the Seventy, Dad associated with them on a daily basis. He was a "Scribe to the Prophets," as were William Clayton, Wilford Woodruff, Joseph F. Smith, William F. Gibbs, Joseph Anderson, and others.

"I am their witness"

When Dad was sustained as a General Authority in April of 1986, after many years serving as the faithful scribe for the Presidents of the Church, he said:

> The Church is led by prophets, seers and revelators. I am their witness. I testify that they are honorable, upright, dedicated men of integrity, committed to teaching the principles of the gospel, who strive with all of their might to prepare a people ready for the return of the head of the Church, Jesus Christ, at His second coming.

This work, *Remembering Seven Prophets*, shares many unique stories, anecdotes, insights, and testimonies about the last seven Presidents of the Church, which are nowhere else available.

I offer this work for the enlightenment and inspiration of the reader and as a tribute to the memory of the seven Presidents of the Church featured in these pages. I love and honor these great men and add my witness to that of my father that they were and are Prophets of God!

Daniel Bay Gibbons
January 1, 2015
Holladay, Utah

CHRONOLOGY OF THE LIFE OF PRESIDENT EZRA TAFT BENSON

August 4, 1899
Ezra Taft Benson is born in Whitney, Idaho, to George T. Benson, Jr., and Sarah Dunkley.

1918
Ezra Taft Benson contracts influenza while in military training in Logan, Utah.

July 1921
Ezra Taft Benson is set apart as a full-time missionary to Great Britain.

1924
Ezra Taft Benson transfers to Brigham Young University following his return from his mission.

Spring of 1926
Ezra Taft Benson graduates with honors from Brigham Young University and is voted Most Popular Man on campus.

July 12, 1926
Ezra Taft Benson and Flora Amussen announce their engagement.

September 10, 1926
Ezra Taft Benson and Flora Amussen are sealed in the Salt Lake Temple by Elder Orson F. Whitney of the Quorum of the Twelve.

July 1927
Ezra Taft Benson and his wife return to Whitney, Idaho, after spending a year doing postgraduate work in agriculture at Iowa State University.

Spring 1928
Ezra Taft Benson and his family move to Preston, Idaho, where he is appointed as agricultural agent for Franklin County.

1929
Ezra Taft Benson moves his family to Boise, Idaho, where he becomes an agricultural economist at the University of Idaho and a specialist for the State of Idaho.

1936
Ezra Taft Benson is given a fellowship grant to study at the University of California at Berkeley. He is appointed to the high council in California, though he had not been released from serving in the stake presidency in Boise.

November 27, 1938
Ezra Taft Benson is sustained as president of the Boise Stake.

January 1939
After counseling with the General Authorities of the Church, Ezra Taft Benson accepts an appointment as the executive secretary of the National Council of Farm Cooperatives in Washington, D.C. This necessitates his release as stake president in Boise.

March 26, 1939
Ezra Taft Benson is released as president of the Boise Stake to enable him to move to Washington D.C. with his family.

June 1940
Ezra Taft Benson is called as the first president of the Washington D.C. Stake.

July 26, 1943
While traveling through Salt Lake City, Ezra Taft Benson is told that President Heber J. Grant wants to visit with him. At a cabin in Emigration Canyon, President Grant calls President Benson as a member of the Quorum of the Twelve.

October 7, 1943
Elder Ezra Taft Benson is ordained and set apart as a member of the Quorum of the Twelve.

March 5, 1944
Elder Ezra Taft Benson is released as president of the Washington D.C. Stake and resigns as the executive secretary of the National Council of Farm Cooperatives. The Bensons then move to Salt Lake City, where he begins his service in the Quorum of the Twelve.

January 29, 1946
Elder Ezra Taft Benson leaves Salt Lake City to serve for eleven months in Europe to help oversee relief efforts given to Church members in the wake of World War II.

August 1947
Elder Ezra Taft Benson gives a talk to the American Institute of Cooperation, which brings him into political prominence with members of the national Republican Party.

1948
During the 1948 U.S. Presidential campaign, New York Governor Thomas E. Dewey seeks advice from Ezra Taft Benson on farming and other matters.

November 1952
U.S. President-elect Dwight D. Eisenhower asks Elder Ezra Taft Benson if he will accept an appointment as Secretary of Agriculture in his new administration.

October 18, 1963
Elder Ezra Taft Benson is called to preside over the European Mission. He spends two years in Europe.

December 1973
When President Harold B. Lee dies unexpectedly, Elder Ezra Taft Benson becomes the President of the Quorum of the Twelve.

November 5, 1985
President Spencer W. Kimball passes away.

November 10, 1985
President Ezra Taft Benson is ordained and set apart as the thirteenth President of the Church.

August 1992
President Ezra Taft Benson's wife, Flora Amussen Benson, passes away in Salt Lake City.

May 30, 1994
President Ezra Taft Benson, thirteenth President of The Church of Jesus Christ of Latter-day Saints, dies at age 94.

"A PORTRAIT OF PRESIDENT BENSON"

It is not difficult for me to create a word portrait of President Ezra Taft Benson, who was one of the most fascinating, complex, whole-souled, and genuine people I have ever met.

I first met Elder Ezra Taft Benson on Thursday, April 9, 1970. On that day I had been greatly surprised to be invited to meet in the early morning hours with the three members of the First Presidency of the Church. At the time I was a Salt Lake City attorney with a very busy law practice. I walked over to the Church Administration Building alone that morning before going to my law office for the day. I was ushered into the council room and introduced to the First Presidency: Joseph Fielding Smith, Harold B. Lee, and N. Eldon Tanner. I then had the most significant interview of my life, the upshot of which was that I was asked by the First Presidency of the Church to give up my legal career and commence serving immediately as the secretary to the First Presidency. I told them I would, and my life was forever changed.

A few minutes later I walked to the Salt Lake Temple with the First Presidency and went with them to the fourth floor Council Room. As the four of us walked into the room, the members of the Quorum of the Twelve stood in front of their upholstered chairs, which were arranged in a semicircle facing the west, where there stood the empty chairs of the First Presidency and a desk for the secretary to the First Presidency. I was then taken around the circle by President Harold B. Lee and introduced to each member of the Twelve, shaking hands with them as I went. Second in seniority in the Twelve was Elder Ezra Taft Benson, then seventy-one years of age.

My first impressions of Ezra Taft Benson were profound, and they altered several false preconceptions I had about him. It is interesting how a close association with a man or woman has the power to alter the opinions we might have about them beforehand. Before my close acquaintance with President Benson, I had always viewed him as a rather austere, no-nonsense man with a perpetually serious expression on his countenance. This may have been due to the serious, never humorous, content of his public sermons. When I first met him on April 9, 1970, he shook my hand warmly and looked with great kindness into my eyes. Indeed, on that occasion President Benson showed toward me an attitude and demeanor that characterized all of our personal relationships during the succeeding decades—he was open, friendly, and cordial. There was nothing feigned or phony or forced in his interaction. He was genuine and wholehearted. Indeed, over the years I have come to believe that the major quality in President Benson's makeup is that he is genuine and whole souled.

So that is a portrait of one of the most unique and fascinating men I have ever met—a man whom I love and sustain as a Prophet, Seer, and Revelator!

Over time, my impressions of President Benson sharpened and deepened. As I began to observe him at close hand—day by day, over a period of months, then years, then decades—I saw that he was actually a man of great humility. This caught me by surprise, as he had served in the leading councils of both the Church and the U.S. government. But despite this, he was wholly without pretension. He was very friendly and outgoing. In private settings he never showed the stridency and austerity that seemed to come through when he preached in public on doctrinal or on political themes.

"His birth was considered a great miracle"

President Ezra Taft Benson often spoke with awe of his mother, Sarah Dunkley Benson, who bore him on August 4, 1899. President Benson was the oldest of eleven children born by his mother. In his long life she took on something of the quality of a saint or a guardian angel.

President Benson almost didn't survive. His birth was a considered a great miracle in the Benson family. He was delivered by a local medical doctor, with his two grandmothers assisting as midwives. The future Prophet and his mother both almost lost their lives during the delivery. He was so large at birth—almost twelve pounds—that the doctor almost despaired of saving the mother. Crude birthing instruments, such as were used in the nineteenth century, were employed and did much damage both to mother and child. After the long and excruciating delivery, the big baby boy emerged bloody and lifeless. The doctor set the infant's body aside, thinking that he had not survived the birth, and turned all his attention upon the mother, who was hemorrhaging terribly. The two grandmothers took the lifeless baby boy into the next room where they bathed him alternately in warm and cold water. Soon the doctor was surprised to hear lusty cries from the next room.

"Two Prophets Walked Out of the Same Farmland"

President Benson was born and raised in the tiny Mormon settlement of Whitney, Idaho. Named after Mormon Apostle Orson F. Whitney, it had a population of only a few hundred people. A few miles away in the equally tiny village of Clifton, another future Prophet—President Harold B. Lee—had been born a few months before President Benson's birth. It is remarkable that in this vast worldwide Church, two future Church Presidents should have been born in the same year and in the same remote and obscure farming community. Two Prophets walked out of the same farmland, as it were. Both boys in their teen years attended the Oneida Stake Academy located in Preston, Idaho. There they became great friends. In those days President Benson went by the nickname "T" and President Lee went by the nickname "Hal."

"T" and "Hal" had much in common aside from their common birth and upbringing in rural Idaho. Both of them went on to serve missions in England. Both married remarkable women who brought out the best in their husbands. Both had a flair for public life and served in political office, President Lee as a Salt Lake City Commissioner and President Benson as the U.S. Secretary of Agriculture. And both were called at relatively young ages to the Quorum of the Twelve, where they went through a decades-long process of refining and tutoring in the presence of great men.

"HE BECAME A MAN AT AGE TWELVE"

As the oldest of eleven children, President Benson had to grow up fast. His early life was filled with farm duties—caring for horses, cows, chickens, and pigs; and hoeing, planting, irrigating, weeding, and harvesting. He followed his father around the farm like a little shadow, always willing to work and to learn. And amid all of this labor, there was the daily chore of milking the cows. Milking was either a never-ending burden or a delight. For young Ezra Taft Benson it was a delight, and never a burden. Little Ezra Taft Benson took to farm life naturally. He always said that he loved hard work. As a boy, his only life aspiration was to become a successful farmer, like his father before him.

When Ezra Taft Benson turned twelve, his father was called as a full-time missionary to labor in the Northern States. This was not uncommon in the period, to call a mature married man to leave his family and occupation to serve in the ministry, though the practice placed heavy burdens upon the families left behind. As the oldest child in a large family, Ezra Taft Benson assumed the workload of a grown man when his father departed. He assumed the daily responsibility of caring for the family's dairy herd. He became a man at age twelve.

"BUNKMATES ON EITHER SIDE OF HIM DIED"

When the United States declared war on Germany and the other Axis powers in 1917, Ezra Taft Benson felt an immediate urge to join the military. He counseled with his parents, and it was decided that he should leave the Oneida Stake Academy and enroll in a military training program at Utah State University in Logan, Utah. He signed the necessary papers and traveled to Logan to begin his training. He lived in a military-style barracks on campus with other new recruits, most of whom were from farming communities in the Cache Valley.

In the fall of 1917, the directors of the military camp decided to give the recruits a two-week leave to return home to their farms to help with the harvest. An announcement was made to the recruits.

The day before the recruits were to return home, Ezra awoke in the morning with a powerful spiritual prompting that he should go home immediately and not wait for the next day. He resisted the prompting and went about his training and military duties as usual, but had the prompting a second and then a third time. He went to his training officer and asked for special permission to return home a day early. Permission was given to him. He left the military camp and caught a ride north to Whitney, where he arrived home about noon.

Later the same day, young Ezra developed a very high fever, and he became delirious. The doctors diagnosed that he was stricken with influenza, which was then sweeping the world in a deadly epidemic. For several days he lay in bed, drifting in and out of consciousness. In one of the moments when he was conscious, he heard the doctor saying that everything had been done medically for the boy, and that only the power of God could save his life. He was then aware of his father and grandfather laying hands upon his head to anoint and bless him.

After receiving a priesthood blessing, President Benson's fever broke, and he began to recover. He later learned that the day he left the military camp, an influenza outbreak had affected most of his fellow recruits. His bunkmates on either side of him died. He lost many friends, including his cousin, George B. Parkinson. Ezra Taft Benson always believed that the spiritual prompting he had received to leave the camp a day early had saved his life.

"A BEAUTIFUL GIRL DROVE BY IN A SPORTS CAR"

After President Benson recovered fully from the influenza in 1918, he enrolled full time as a student at Utah State Agricultural College. He had saved his money and, with the support of his parents, he made preparations to move back to Logan for the school year. While on a visit to the campus to make his final preparations, he was with a group of friends, walking along the street. A beautiful girl drove by in a sports car. The boys watched the girl drive away, and then were surprised when "T" Benson, as he was called then, turned to his friends and announced that this was the girl he would marry some day! They laughed at him because the girl was Flora Amussen, a member of a very wealthy family who was also one of the most popular and beautiful girls at the college. The thought that "T" Benson, a farm boy from Whitney would stand a chance with the beautiful and accomplished Flora Amussen was beyond imagination.

Not long after seeing Flora Amussen for the first time, Ezra was shocked when she appeared in his Sunday School class in little Whitney, Idaho. Flora was the weekend guest of his cousin, Ann Dunkley. Then Ann's father asked Ezra if he would mind driving the two girls on an outing to Lava Hot Springs that afternoon. Ezra agreed immediately, and then arranged to have someone handle his evening milking chores. During the drive to and from Lava Hot Springs, Ezra and Flora got acquainted. Ezra discovered that despite an upbringing of privilege and wealth, Flora was outgoing, modest, and humble. He became very interested in this girl.

Once Ezra settled in Logan for the school year and started his studies, he began to date Flora Amussen, and their relationship blossomed over the next two years. Then Ezra received a mission call to serve in Great Britain in 1921. After being set apart for his mission, he traveled with his fellow missionaries from Salt Lake City to Ogden, Utah, where the main train lines ran. Flora Amussen traveled with them, and on the train trip they had a talk about their future. During his mission they had what was then called an "understanding." They understood that, in all likelihood, they would one day be married.

"OUR BENSON"

Ezra Taft Benson served his full-time mission in England at a time when the Church faced great opposition. For example, a lurid silent film entitled *Trapped by the Mormons* was released in 1922 and then shown throughout England by ministers of the Church of England to deter their parishioners from giving the young Mormon missionaries a listening ear. The movie portrayed the young missionaries as degenerates who were trying to lure women to Utah for immoral purposes.

I have often thought that this unprecedented spirit of opposition was a great training ground for young Ezra Taft Benson, as it would also be for his fellow Cache Valley farm friend, Harold B. Lee. It taught him that the work could move forward despite fierce opposition. It also taught him patience in the face of unrelenting personal attacks.

In the mission field Ezra Taft Benson fell under the sway of two great leaders of the Church. His first mission president was Elder Orson F. Whitney of the Quorum of the Twelve. The older Apostle was to have a great influence upon the spiritual life of the young missionary. Ezra Taft Benson was electrified when he heard Elder Whitney's testimony of having seen the Savior in a vision. It had a profound effect upon the young man's life. Later Elder Whitney. would perform the marriage ceremony of young Elder Benson to his wife, Flora Amussen.

President Whitney first assigned Ezra Taft Benson to labor in the city of Carlisle in the Newcastle District. A short time later, President Whitney was released and replaced by a young mission president, David O. McKay. President McKay transferred Ezra Taft Benson from Carlisle to Sunderland, where he served as the conference clerk and branch president in the Sunderland Branch. President McKay was a second great leader who was to have a lasting impact upon Ezra Taft Benson's life. In Sunderland, under the leadership of President McKay, Elder Benson began teaching the saints the then-novel concept of "every member a missionary." He also began counseling the saints not to immigrate to America, but to remain in place in their branches in England to build up the Church locally. Ezra Taft Benson completed his mission serving as branch president in Sunderland and was much beloved by the

British saints, who often called him, "our Benson!"

"THE YOUNG COUPLE DECIDED AGAINST MARRYING"

Following his return from the mission field, President Benson received permission to tour for a month in Europe with another missionary, and then returned home. Passing through Salt Lake City on his way home to Whitney, Idaho, he received a special blessing from the Church patriarch, who promised him that he would live to a "goodly age" and that his name would be held in "honorable remembrance" throughout all time.

Back in Logan, he picked up his studies at Utah State and also his relationship with Flora Amussen, who had waited for him during his mission to England. Interestingly, the young couple decided against marrying at that point, and instead decided that Flora should serve a full-time mission of her own. She was called to the Hawaii Mission, and President Benson now took his turn waiting for her to return. During her mission he transferred to Brigham Young University, where he graduated with honors in 1926, the same year in which he married Flora upon her return from Hawaii.

"A STRIKING CONTRAST"

There was a striking contrast between the backgrounds of President Ezra Taft Benson and Sister Flora Amussen Benson. Sister Flora Benson was the daughter of Carl Christian Amussen, a wealthy Salt Lake jeweler. Her father died when she was still a baby, but left her mother, Barbara Smith Amussen a substantial legacy, and little Flora grew up amid wealth and comfort. She was raised in an urban home of privilege, culture, and refinement. She enjoyed many of the good things of life. For example, when President Benson first laid eyes upon his future wife, she was driving a little sports car around the college town of Logan, Utah. She was an expert tennis player, winning Utah State University's women's singles titles. In short, she was everything that the country boy, "T" Benson, was not—well educated, cultured, and refined. He had been raised on a farm, the oldest in a large family, where all had to work hard merely to survive.

President Benson often commented upon his wife's superior upbringing and jokingly made mention of the fact that he had "married up." But despite his humble upbringing, President Benson was a man of great native ability who had the potential to be molded into someone of achievement. In that sense, Sister Benson was in no way superior to her husband, but she became the catalyst for him to reach toward heights of education and culture he might not otherwise have sought. This impression that President Benson was a man of superior native ability was universally shared by those in the Church who knew and loved him.

"AN EXEMPLARY LATTER-DAY SAINT FAMILY"

President Benson did post-graduate work at both Iowa State University and at the University of California at Berkeley. Later, he accepted a position with the National Council of Farm Cooperatives in Washington D.C. During each of these moves, Flora and his children accompanied him. In each place they lived, they lived the standards of an exemplary Latter-day Saint family, with family prayer, family home evening, and daily scripture study being strictly observed.

In each place they went, Ezra Taft Benson was also called upon for significant Church service. For example, he served as a counselor in a stake presidency and then a stake president in Boise, Idaho, and then as a stake president in Washington, D.C.

"The Scoutmaster Shaved His Head"

The wards of the Oneida Stake at the north end of the Cache Valley were among the earliest sponsors of the Boy Scouts of America. Ezra Taft Benson was a boy scout as a young man and a lifelong proponent of the program for boys and young men. He later became the scoutmaster in the Whitney Ward and was what we may call a "youth man," always willing to help the young people of the Church in their activity programs.

As an old man, the subject of scouting was seldom mentioned without his reminiscence about serving as a scoutmaster with the boys from Whitney. He was especially fond of recalling a special troop outing that included a hike over the mountain to Bear Lake. The hike was a reward for the boys' winning a singing competition. Because of a dare, all of the boys wore their hair short in what was then called a "crew cut," while the scoutmaster, Ezra Taft Benson, shaved his head completely for the trek. The camaraderie he built with the boys of his troop lasted a lifetime.

As one of the senior leaders of the Church, Ezra Taft Benson was a tireless proponent for the Church's continuation of its sponsorship of the Boy Scouts of America, and he received some of scouting's most distinguished awards.

"THE CABIN ITSELF WAS A SACRED PLACE"

During the hottest weeks of the summer, President Heber J. Grant often traveled up Emigration Canyon to a small cabin, where he spent many happy and pleasant days. The cabin was rustic, with a stone fireplace heating a large living room. There was a small bedroom adjoining the living room, where President Grant slept. Here the Prophet was not far from downtown Salt Lake City and could transact Church business during daylight hours and receive visitors, and at night he could enjoy the utter peace and quiet and the invigorating coolness of the mountains.

On July 26, 1943, President Grant was staying in his cabin in Emigration Canyon when he invited forty-four-year-old Ezra Taft Benson to visit him in the canyon. There, in a private room, he extended a call to the younger man to serve in the Quorum of the Twelve. President Benson often spoke about the sacredness of this moment when he was interviewed privately by the Prophet and called to the Apostleship. For President Benson, the cabin itself was also a sacred place—a place where his entire life was changed and reshaped.

A few months after he was called and ordained as the thirteenth President of the Church, President Benson made arrangements to visit the old cabin in Emigration Canyon where President Grant had called him to the Twelve. The cabin was then owned by the Cannon family, and they invited President Benson and his family to visit. President Benson went alone into the little bedroom adjoining the living room. He closed the door and spent some time alone. He then invited his family to join him, and they sat for a long time reminiscing about how the call from President Grant had altered the lives of the Benson family during the nearly forty-five years that had intervened since his call in 1943. Those years had taken President Benson around the world in the service of the Church, to Washington, D.C., where he served in the highest councils of government, and back home to Salt Lake City, where he ultimately became President of the Church.

"CITIES LEVELED BY INTENSE BOMBING"

For nearly a year following World War II, President Benson lived in Europe, where he directed the administration of relief to Latter-day Saints affected by the war. He established a headquarters in London, England, and then made numerous trips throughout Europe. He often spoke of his shock at the devastation that had occurred in Europe as a result of the war, particularly in Germany. All of the major cities had essentially been leveled by intense Allied bombing, and hundreds of thousands, even millions, of people were displaced. He organized the Church's efforts to distribute welfare commodities shipped from the United States to the destitute and scattered saints. He also worked to supervise the finding of lost members of the Church and to strengthen and train local leaders and missionaries.

In later years, President Benson spoke often of his hatred of dictatorships, which arose from what he observed firsthand in Europe in 1946 to 1947. It explains much about his great, energized attacks upon Communism in the years ahead. It was also during this period that he came to the attention of prominent Republicans in Washington, D.C. It was this prominence that caused his name to surface in 1952 as a possible member of President-elect Dwight D. Eisenhower's Cabinet.

"IF THE INVITATION COMES IN THE PROPER SPIRIT, YOU OUGHT TO ACCEPT"

After General Dwight D. Eisenhower. was elected as the U.S. President in November of 1952, Elder Ezra Taft Benson was asked if he would accept an appointment as the Secretary of Agriculture. Because Elder Benson served as a member of the Quorum of the Twelve, he counseled with President David O. McKay about the request. President Benson told me that President McKay was initially hesitant about the request, and suggested that he wait to decide until he had met with President-elect Eisenhower in person. The counsel the Prophet gave to Elder Benson was that "if the invitation comes in the proper spirit, you ought to accept."

Elder Benson subsequently flew to New York, where he had a private interview with President Eisenhower. President Eisenhower told Elder Benson that should he accept the appointment, he would never be asked to promote any policy with which he disagreed. Given the spirit in which the appointment was made, Elder Benson accepted.

"A MODERN-DAY JOSEPH IN PHARAOH'S KINGDOM"

I, along with many thousands of other Latter-day Saints, watched with great interest in the weeks following the election when President Eisenhower named Elder Ezra Taft Benson of the Quorum of the Twelve to a post in his Cabinet as Secretary of Agriculture. Many members of the Church watched Elder Benson's career in Washington with great interest. Many people shared his conservative views and admired his integrity, intelligence, and hard work. He and his family were good exemplars of a Latter-day Saint family, and generally the Church membership basked in the glow of Elder Benson's service and reputation.

Brother D. Arthur Haycock, who served as a private secretary to several Presidents of the Church, also served for several years on Elder Benson's staff in Washington, D.C., during the years of the Eisenhower Administration. Arthur had some significant insights into President Benson's years in Washington, D.C., which he often shared with me. According to Arthur, Elder Benson began his service as the

Secretary of Agriculture with the thought that he was in a sense a modern-day Joseph, elevated to a high position in Pharaoh's Kingdom, to fill the granaries of the United States against the day of famine.

"To open doors for the Church"

My sense is that President Benson's years in Washington, D.C. had a profound impact upon the man. It opened up avenues of worldly influence to him that had never before been open to a Mormon, let alone to a General Authority. While in Washington, President Benson made hundreds of contacts, including contacts with foreign heads of state, which would ultimately be of great help to the Church in the years to come.

President Benson was aware of his influence, and he used it carefully for the blessing of the work. He knew that politics and influence could open doors for the Church. Even decades after his withdrawal from government service, the topic of politics and government leaders, past and present, continued to occupy his conversation. In about 1971, a few months after I began my work with the First Presidency of the Church, Elder Benson invited me to pay a visit to his office. He was pleased to show me the chair, the government flags, the photographs, and other memorabilia brought from his office in Washington. He spoke of his time with

President Dwight D. Eisenhower and about the man's character. He called my attention to a picture of Eisenhower's Cabinet and discussed it for a long time, commenting on the personalities of the various members. All this he did without an air of condescension or pride, but in a matter-of-fact manner. This experience of sitting in the leading councils of both the Church and the U.S. government was simply a part of President Benson's makeup. It was a part of "who he was."

Years after this first visit to President Benson's private office, I gained further insight into the effect of his years of service in the U.S. Cabinet. There was an aura of stature and notoriety that this service gave to President Benson and the Church, which lingered for many years. He was a celebrity, both in and out of the Church, and he knew very well how to make good use of his celebrity. He seemed determined to use his experience and status as a former Cabinet member for the good of the Church. For example, he was always ready to use that card to open doors to people of significance who might help the cause of the Church. He seemed to feel that the Lord had placed the tools of status and influence into his hands, and he was determined to use it to advance his work as a minister of the gospel and a representative of the Church.

An example of this special influence occurred in the late 1960's, almost a decade after President Benson concluded his service in the Cabinet. Former Israeli Prime Minister David Ben Gurion contacted Ezra Taft Benson in Salt Lake City and invited the Apostle to pay him a visit in Israel. David Ben Gurion had heard of Orson Hyde's dedication of the Holy Land for the return of the Jews in 1841. He wanted a copy of the dedicatory prayer for a history of Israel he was writing, and to discuss it with a Mormon of stature who could explain it to him. President Benson paid the great Israeli patriot a visit in Israel and had a lengthy discussion with him. David Ben Gurion told President Benson that the Mormon people seemed to understand the Jews better than anyone else on earth.

On another occasion, in the late 1970's, President Benson was asked to make contact with some of his long-time Egyptian contacts on behalf of the Church in an effort to obtain recognition for the Church there. All of this opened doors for the Church in both Israel and Egypt and in many other parts of the world, due in part to the former government service and reputation of Ezra Taft Benson.

"HE CULTIVATED A SENSE OF FAMILY"

As the Secretary of Agriculture, Ezra Taft Benson directed one of the largest departments in the U.S. government, with tens of thousands of employees located around the world. In order to survive administratively, he had to become a master leader and to delegate broadly. He brought this skill of strong administration with him when he became the President of the Quorum of the Twelve and then later as the thirteenth President of the Church. His ability to delegate freed him from administrative detail and gave him freedom to see the broad direction of the Church and to chart a safe course. It also allowed his Brethren to develop as they grew under the weight of delegated responsibility. With this skill, he also cultivated a sense of family among those who worked with him. He treated all of his fellow laborers as family. He took a genuine interest in those who made up his inner circle, often expressing his love and appreciation for them and going out of his way to perform thoughtful acts of service.

"HE LEARNED TO THINK ON HIS FEET"

President Benson was one of the most eloquent speakers among the General Authorities of the Church. His speaking skill was first honed when he served as a young missionary in England. There he learned to think on his feet as he spoke to unruly crowds on street corners. He also gained extensive experience in public speaking as he served in various teaching and executive positions in the Church. Then during his Washington years as a member of the U.S. Cabinet, he learned poise under pressure as he jousted with Presidents, Senators, Congressmen, bureaucrats, and lobbyists in the Capitol, and with politicians out on the hustings. Regardless of the forum in which he spoke, he was always earnest, sincere, and articulate. He conveyed the impression of being absolutely honest and above board. He could be very blunt sometimes, especially when he was speaking about communism or moral transgression. Usually, however, he was very positive and upbeat in his speaking.

"HE OCCASIONALLY TOLD A GOOD STORY"

Despite his formal and earnest manner as a speaker at the pulpit, in private settings President Ezra Taft Benson was warm, friendly, and even humorous. Unlike many popular Church speakers, President Benson seldom, if ever, used humor in speaking. But in private he enjoyed a good laugh and occasionally told a good story. Here are three of my favorite stories shared by President Benson:

On one occasion, President Benson shared this story in private to a small group of his close associates: When a man boasted to his wife that he had been promoted to vice president in his company, she seemed unimpressed. "Why, there is even a vice president in charge of prunes at the supermarket," she said. Doubting her word, the husband later called the supermarket and asked to speak to the vice president in charge of prunes. "Packaged or bulk?" asked the voice.

President Benson shared this story one day at the dinner table: He told about the man who insisted that his wife serve only margarine at the table because butter had become too expensive. Once, while guests were being treated to butter at the family table, one of the sons, weary of margarine, went into the kitchen and brought in a plate of butter, which he then helped himself to, spreading it lavishly on his bread. Startled, the boys' father, hoping to restrain and instruct his son, observed that the butter cost sixty cents a pound. Undeterred, the boy answered, "For butter, I would say it's very well worth it."

President Benson once told me this very amusing story: When a man who had died presented himself at the Pearly Gates, the attendant there asked to see his temple recommend. The man promptly excused himself and said he would be right back. He was gone a very long time and when he returned the attendant asked what had taken so long. "I have been looking all over hell for my bishop," the man answered.

"WE'LL SEE IF YOUR SPIRITUAL ANTENNA IS UP"

In 1970 I had a memorable personal spiritual experience involving Elder Ezra Taft Benson, who was then a member of the Quorum of the Twelve. I recount it because it shows the miraculous way in which the Spirit works with the leading Brethren of the Church, and it also reveals something of the character of President Benson.

At the time of this experience Russell M. Nelson, now a member of the Twelve, was then the President of the Bonneville Stake where my wife and I resided with our family. It was stake conference weekend, and the General Authority visitor was Elder Benson. During the general session, I was sitting with my wife, Helen, and our children in the chapel. President Nelson stood up and announced that Elder Benson now had a special matter of business to transact. At that moment, I had an impression that Elder Benson would call Harold Bennett, a long-time member of our stake, as a stake patriarch. Impulsively I leaned over and whispered that impression to Helen who was seated beside me, who looked at me skeptically and responded, "We'll see if your spiritual antenna is up this morning." I'm sure that part of her skepticism arose from the fact that we already had a stake patriarch and there was no reason to expect a second to be called, sustained, and ordained. Elder Benson walked to the pulpit and amid gasps of surprise and murmurs of approval from the congregation, presented the name of Harold Bennett as an additional stake patriarch. Helen and I exchanged a meaningful glance. We both knew that for some reason the Spirit had given me a true flash of inspiration about this surprise call.

Later in the same meeting, the new patriarch, Harold Bennett, was called on to speak by President Russell M. Nelson. In his remarks, the new patriarch told, in substance, this story: "Several years ago as I rode home alone from work one evening, a voice spoke to me and said, 'LeGrand Richards will be called as the new member of the Twelve.' When I got home, I went into the kitchen where my wife Emily was preparing the evening meal. I hugged her and then said, 'Emily. I know who the new member of the Twelve will be.' 'Oh?' she answered. 'Who is it?' I told her it would be LeGrand Richards. 'Oh, you must be mistaken, Hal,' she responded. 'LeGrand Richards is the Presiding Bishop. The Brethren surely wouldn't call him.' I told her, 'Well, that's what the voice said.' LeGrand Richards was, indeed, called to the Twelve as the voice had told me. Then this morning, in the interval between the time the phone rang at our home and the time I answered it, that same voice said to me, 'You will be called by Elder Ezra Taft Benson as a patriarch.' On the line was President Russell M. Nelson who said that Elder Benson wanted to talk to me privately at the stake center. When I came here, Elder Benson called me as a patriarch."

This experience occurred not long after I was called to work as the secretary to the First Presidency. A few days following this incident, I happened to be at work visiting with Elder Benson, and I mentioned the impression I had had at the previous Sunday's stake conference. He listened with great interest, and then told me, "The decision to call another patriarch was not made until early Sunday morning. There were several men under consideration. Then the clear prompting came to me that it was to be Harold Bennett." Elder Benson told me that this was an illustration of the truth of the work. It shows that the Spirit is at work both among the leaders of the Church as well as with ordinary saints. He said that it reminded him of the teaching of the Prophet Joseph Smith, that "God hath not revealed anything to Joseph, but what he will make known unto the Twelve, and even the least Saint may know all things as fast as he is able to bear them" (*Teachings of the Prophet Joseph Smith*).

"COOPERATION BETWEEN TWO FUTURE CHURCH PRESIDENTS"

During President Kimball's final months of life, when President Gordon B. Hinckley was the only physically active member of the First Presidency, President Benson developed a special relationship with President Hinckley. It was a powerful lesson to see President Benson give such deference and respect to his position as a counselor in the First Presidency. At the same time, President Hinckley had the wisdom to counsel often with President Benson, who he knew at any moment could become the senior Apostle upon the death of President Kimball. It was an interesting time to observe this, and it strengthened my estimation of the qualities of followership and leadership in President Ezra Taft Benson.

President Gordon B. Hinckley directed the Church by delegation of authority for many months while Presidents Spencer W. Kimball and Marion G. Romney were not well. He handled it efficiently but not without trauma. One aspect of the work that troubled him especially was considering the cases of cancellation of temple sealings, divorce clearances, and the restoration of blessings. Ordinarily these matters were heard by the full First Presidency, but with President Kimball and Romney physically unable to be in the office, President Hinckley sat alone in the consideration of these heavy matters, with only me at his side as his scribe and secretary. He often told me how uncomfortable he felt in handling these matters alone and sensed the need for additional counsel in deciding them. At that point he began to invite President Benson to join us each Tuesday morning for this purpose. This practice continued for many months until the time of President Kimball's death. Although seven years older than he, with almost twenty years of seniority in the Apostleship and with vastly greater experience in international affairs, President Benson was always perfectly subordinate to President Hinckley through all the months of this unusual relationship. President Benson showed that same deference when counseling with the Twelve and with the other General Authorities.

President Hinckley also looked to President Benson for leadership and direction in other areas during this same time period. With both President Kimball and President

Romney often unwell and out of the office, it was only natural, as President Benson was senior to him in the Apostleship and would likely become the next President of the Church. For example, President Hinckley called in President Benson for counsel in purchasing properties for future temples.

This cooperation between two future Presidents of the Church, Ezra Taft Benson and Gordon B. Hinckley, was a great testimony builder for me. It showed the wisdom and leadership of both men, as well as their Christlike attributes of kindness and patience. This manner of leadership and followership adds great stability to the administration of the Church and demonstrates the wisdom of a policy whereby the senior Apostle succeeds to leadership on the death or disability of the Prophet.

"THE PROPHETIC MANTLE"

Those of us who worked closely with President Ezra Taft Benson at the time of his ordination as the thirteenth President of the Church were all inspired by the way in which the prophetic mantle quickly fell upon him. From the day of his ordination, he was greatly magnified.

It is interesting that many of the themes President Benson emphasized during his tenure as President emerged in his private conversations and in his public sermons in the earliest days and weeks after his ordination. For example, in every conversation or discussion and in every sermon he gave in those earliest days, I heard him give special emphasis to *The Book of Mormon*. He also went to great lengths in expressing love for everyone. I had witnessed the same phenomenon occur following the ordinations of Presidents Harold B. Lee and Spencer W. Kimball.

"No Empty Chairs"

President Benson had powerful feelings for his family. He was intensely loyal to his family. It was said if you challenged one of the Bensons, you should be prepared to take on the whole family. In times of trial, in times of illness, in times of emergency, they spoke as with a single voice. When job promotions or advancements or moves to this city or that were being considered, the entire family was consulted. An achievement of one member became a cause for celebration by the entire family. And when one of them faced a special task, all joined in to lend support. So when President Benson rose to speak in General Conference, the one sitting at the end of the Benson bench would whisper, "Pray for Dad." That message would be passed from one to the other down the row until all were united in praying for the family patriarch as he stood at the pulpit in the Tabernacle. And if a family friend were seated on the row, he would be temporarily admitted into the Benson prayer chain. A favorite wish expressed by President Benson was that in the hereafter there would be "no empty chairs" in the Benson family circle.

President and Sister Benson enjoyed an unusually close relationship. This became especially evident during the 1970's when Sister Flora Benson began to experience some health problems. I remember that one day Sister Benson was hospitalized, and President Benson called me, asking that her name be placed upon the special prayer roll of the First Presidency and Quorum of the Twelve. He told me that she was feeling very uneasy in the hospital, being separated from President Benson. "She is all right while I am with her," he told me, "but she dreads being alone."

It was President Benson's powerful feeling for his family—past, present and future—which prompted him to direct that he be buried in the little country cemetery overlooking his hometown of Whitney, Idaho. When Sister Flora Benson died in 1992, he had a large headstone prepared which contained all the relevant facts for both of them, except the date of his death. And unlike any other headstone I have ever seen, it also had the names of all of their children carved in stone.

It reminded me of the Prophet Joseph Smith's statement, made at a funeral in Nauvoo:

> I will tell you what I want. If tomorrow I shall be called to lie in yonder tomb, in the morning of the resurrection let me strike hands with my father, and cry, 'My father,' and he will say, 'My son, my son,' as soon as the rock rends and before we come out of our graves. . . . And when the voice calls for the dead to arise, suppose I am laid by the side of my father, what would be the first joy of my heart? To meet my father, my mother, my brother, my sister. (*History of the Church*, 5:361-62).

"What's best for the Kingdom?"

I often heard President Ezra Taft Benson pose this rhetorical question, when faced with questions of importance in the administration of the Church: "What's best for the Kingdom?" If there were ever a significant question about missionary work, temples, family history, Church Welfare, or a myriad other issues, President Benson would often pause before speaking, and ask, "What's best for the Kingdom?" Sometimes the answer he received led to surprising results. After asking this question, he very often laid aside his first, impulsive course of action, and chose something of more lasting value.

This question became a kind of touchstone by which he guided not only the Church, but also his daily walk as a man and a disciple of Jesus Christ. I am confident that he became a better man, husband, father, grandfather, disciple, Church leader, and President of the Church by constantly asking himself, "What's best for the Kingdom?"

"I LOOK UPON YOU AS A TRUE FRIEND"

In the days before I ended my service as the secretary to the First Presidency and was subsequently called to the Seventy, I was privileged to spend several hours with President Benson alone. At the time, President Benson was just commencing his service as the thirteenth President of the Church. During one of our meetings he said to me, in substance, "Brother Gibbons, I am so grateful for what you have done for me. I look upon you as a true friend." On another occasion, I expressed to him the hope that one day I would be able to write his biography, as I had already written biographies of a dozen Presidents of the Church. At the time there was only a single biography of President Benson in print, written by Sheri L. Dew. He referred to this one biography and protested that anyone would ever want a second biography of him. When I expressed the opinion that over time there would be several biographies of him written, he indicated he would be honored to have me write his biography.

"POISE AND SELF-CONTROL"

If I were asked to name President Benson's salient characteristics, I would give this list in order: integrity, perseverance, faith in God and the Church, love of family, and patriotism.

Poise and self-control also appear high on the list. In more than twenty years of personal association with him, in conversations with others who knew him well, and in reviewing voluminous documents about his life while writing his biography, I found or learned of no instance when he allowed his temper or anger to dominate his conduct. I know of many instances when he was heavily provoked, but in no case did he ever lose his temper. He was always in control of himself. His feelings were kept in check. And some of his feelings ran very deep. Elder Joseph Anderson of the Seventy, whom I succeeded as secretary to the First Presidency, told me that he had seen several occasions when Ezra Taft Benson was provoked by strong personal attacks. Elder Anderson said these attacks would have angered and upset almost any man, but they left Ezra Taft Benson completely unruffled.

"No weapon that is formed against thee shall prosper"

President Ezra Taft Benson was a thoughtful, introspective man. He lived very much within himself. My sense is that he had deep-seated thoughts and aspirations that he nourished inside, but which were seldom, if ever, divulged to others, except, perhaps, to members of his own family. And I would not doubt that there were some sacred things that he told to no one, even to his own wife and children.

I gained some insight into his inner world during a three-hour conversation I had with him shortly after his ordination as President of the Church. During that time, he confided to me that he had long carried around in his wallet a piece of paper on which is quoted this scripture:

> No weapon that is formed against thee shall prosper; and every tongue that shall revile against thee in judgment thou shalt condemn. This is the heritage of the servants of the Lord, and their righteousness is of me, saith the Lord. (Isaiah 54:17 and 3 Nephi 22:17)

ABOUT THE AUTHOR

Daniel Bay Gibbons is a writer living in Holladay, Utah. He is a former trial attorney and judge and is the author of three previous books. He has served as a full-time missionary, twice as a bishop, and as president of the Russia Novosibirsk Mission.

INDEX

American Institute of Cooperation, 9
Anderson, Joseph, 3
Ben Gurion, David, 44
Benson, Flora Amussen, 6, 24, 27, 30
    death of, 10, 59
    missionary service, 29
Benson, George T., Jr., 5
Benson, President Ezra Taft, 3
    and Francis M. Gibbons, 62
    and GBH, 54
    and HBL, 18
    and New York Governor Thomas E. Dewey, 9
    and President Dwight D. Eisenhower, 9
    life
        Apostolic service, 8, 9
        birth, 5, 15
        Boy Scouts, 33
        call to Twelve, 8, 35
        childhood, 17, 19
        Church service, 7, 32
        courtship, 25
        death of, 10
        education, 5, 6, 7, 24, 29, 32
        employment, 6, 7, 32
        family, 58
        health problems, 22
        in Europe after WWII, 8

marriage, 6, 30
military, 5
military service, 21
mission, 5
mission to England, 25, 26
patriarchal blessing, 29
political career, 9, 38, 39, 40, 42, 46
President of the Church, 10, 57
President of the Twelve, 9
Secretary of Agriculture, 9
World War II, 37
motto, 61
personal qualities, 11
eloquence, 47
faith, 63
genuineness, 13
humility, 13
integrity, 63
kindness, 13
patriotism, 63
poise and self-control, 63
sense of humor, 48
spirituality, 21, 50
unpretentious, 14
scripture carried in wallet, 64
Benson, Sarah Dunkley, 5, 15
Boise Stake, 7
Boise, Idaho, 6, 32
Bonneville Stake, 50
Boy Scouts of America and ETB, 33
Brigham Young University, 2, 29
Cannon family, 36

Clayton, William, 3
Clifton, Idaho, 17
Council Room in
  Salt Lake Temple,
  12
Dew, Sheri L., 62
Dewey, Governor
  Thomas E., 9
Dunkley, Ann, 25
Egypt
  ETB opens doors
    in, 44
Eisenhower,
  President Dwight
  D., 43
Eisenhower, U.S.
  President Dwight
  D., 9, 38, 39
Emigration Canyon,
  8, 35
European Mission,
  9
Gibbons, Francis
  M.
  and ETB, 62
  as a "Plutarch" to
    the Presidents
    of the Church,
    1
  as secretary to
    the First
    Presidency, 3
  biographies
    written by, 1
  interviews of, 1
  meets ETB, 11
  testimony of the
    Prophets, 3
Gibbs, William F., 3
Grant, President
  Heber J., 35
  calls ETB to
    Twelve, 8
Harold, Bennett
  call as patriarch
    by ETB, 50
Hawaii Mission, 29
Haycock, D. Arthur
  and ETB in
    Washington,
    D.C., 40
Hinckley, President
  Gordon B., 2, 3
  and ETB, 54

Hunter, President Howard W., 3
Hyde, Elder Orson, 44
Iowa State University, 6, 32
Israel
  ETB opens door in, 44
Kimball, President Spencer W.
  and Francis M. Gibbons, 3
  death of, 10
  final years, 54
Lava Hot Springs, 25
Lee, President Harold B., 3, 11
  boyhood friendship with ETB, 17
  death of, 9
Logan, Utah, 5, 21
London, England, 37
McKay, President David O.
  and ETB's appointment to U.S. Cabinet, 39
  mission president to ETB, 27
Monson, President Thomas S., 3
National Council of Farm Cooperatives, 7, 32
Nelson, President Russell M., 50
Ogden, Utah, 25
Oneida Stake, 33
Oneida Stake Academy, 17, 21
Parkinson, George B., 22
Plutarch, 2
Preston, Idaho, 6, 17
Quorum of the Twelve, 8
Republican Party, 9
Salt Lake Temple, 12

Secretary of Agriculture, 39, 46
Secretary to the First Presidency, 11
Seventy, First Quorum of, 3
Smith, President Joseph, 2
Smith, President Joseph F.
  as scribe to the Prophet, 3
Smith, President Joseph Fielding, 3, 11
Tanner, President N. Eldon, 11
Trapped by the Mormons (Anti-Mormon silent film), 26
University of California at Berkeley, 7, 32
University of Idaho, 6
Utah State Agricultural College, 24
Utah State University, 21
Washington D.C. Stake, 7
Washington, D.C., 7, 42
Whitney, Elder Orson F., 6, 17
  and ETB, 26
  vision of the Savior, 27
Whitney, Idaho, 5, 6, 17, 25
Woodruff, President Wilford
  as a scribe to the Prophet, 3
World War II, 8, 37

www.ingramcontent.com/pod-product-compliance
Lightning Source LLC
Chambersburg PA
CBHW071539080526
44588CB00011B/1731